DRAWING
EXTERIORS

DRAWING EXTERIORS

CHAPTER II

CHOOSING A TECHNIQUE FOR THE BUILDING

SECTION 1

So far we have been concentrating on interiors but there are many designers out there who are involved with exterior planning. so how can we cope with that discipline. We are now going to study a number of buildings that we have been associated with and choose a method suitable for that building

THESE TECHNIQUES WOULD ALSO BE USEFUL WHEN PREPARING GRANNY FLATS US STYLE

PROJECT STUDY A

CHAPTER 2

AVIEMORE BUNGALOW

- Our bungalow in Aviemore
- Built by Barratts in the 1980's
- Semi detached 2 bed

While we were at our hotel in Glen Clova we needed a bolt hole to get away from the stress and the strain of day to day management of the hotel and staff plus the numerous demanding promotions

We had already been to Aviemore several times before buying the hotel and fell in love with the then, fresh face of Scottish leisure. Barratts were building and promoting heavily at the time and this was one of our favourite houses.

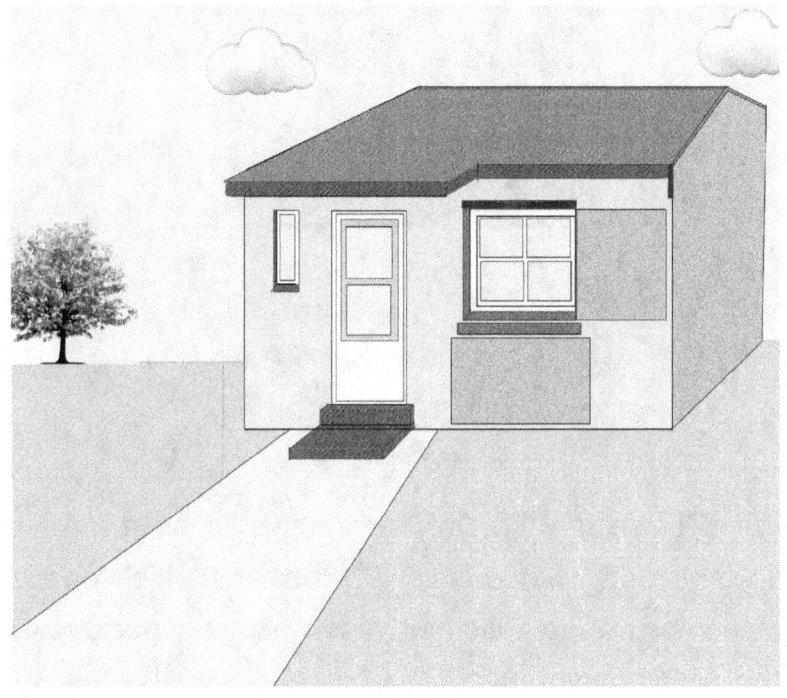

This is our half

Aviemore study

We will use the 1 point perspective technique for this particular study. Sometimes it is obvious which one to use but more often than not it is what you decide would be the best presentation.

You will need to be proficient in 1 point before you start the excercise. If necessary you will need to consult our guides or mini guides - all available on line.

1 point 3d study

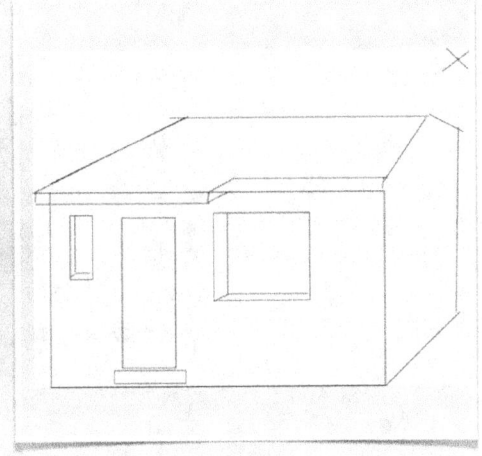

* as usual start with basics

FIX THE VANISHING POINT FOR THE BEST VIEW

BASICALLY IT IS A SIMPLE 1 POINT STUDY

As usual you start with a box then create the building inside the box. You may even wish to actually draw the box to modify.

Aviemore study

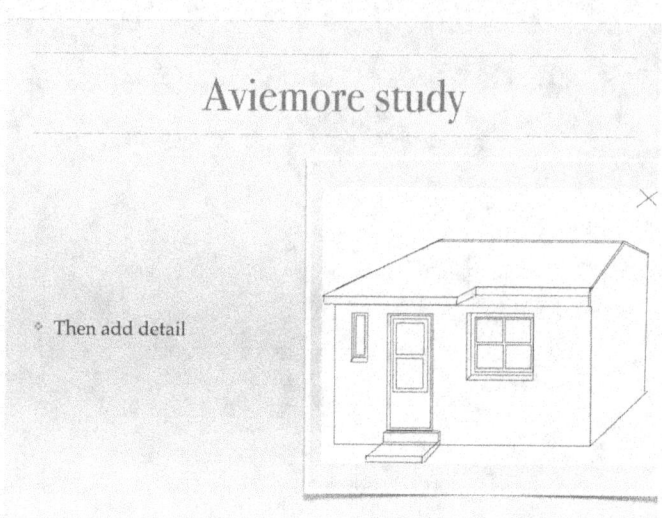

◇ Then add detail

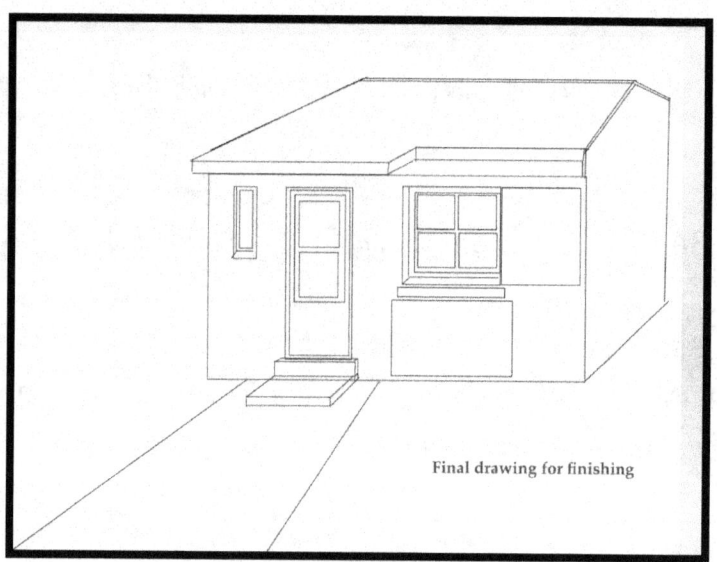

Final drawing for finishing

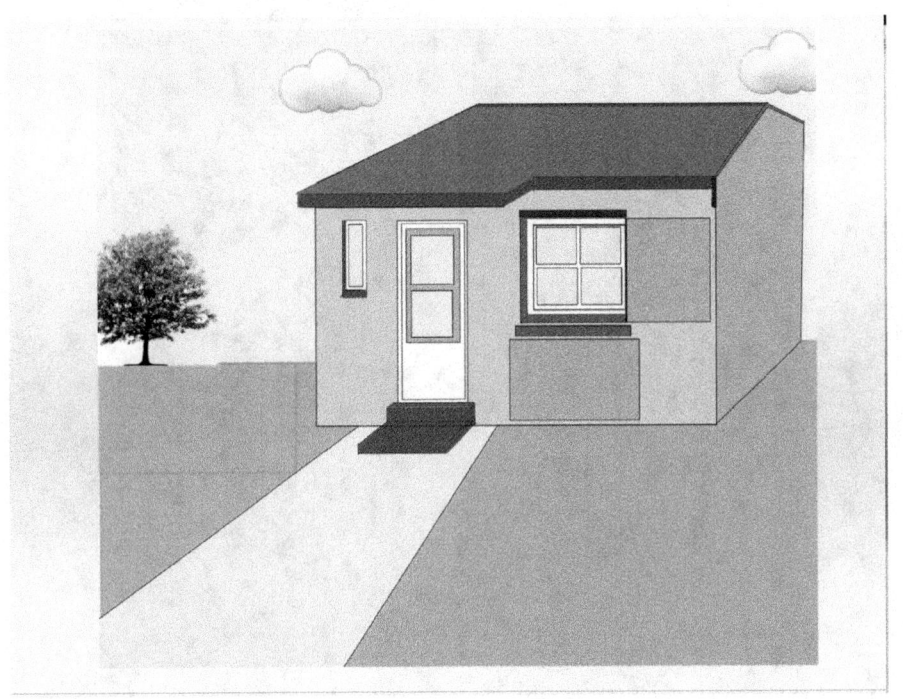

Final rendered drawing with a few extras to enhance the presentation. Even in monochrome this can be quite effective

PROJECT STUDY B
CHAPTER 3

HOUSE IN BILLINGHAM

New 2 bed semi in Teeside
On a new estate
With integral garage
Plus an irritating alarm system

This is our bolt hole in Billingham during our kitchen studio period in Northamptonshire. We had 2 studios and a factory and quite a few staff. This served us well plus we were also developing our training programme charging around the country in our Volkswagen Scirocco. Wonderful car but very uncomfortable. Also very fast. On a trip to Middlesborough to complete the purchase of this house I was stopped by a traffic cop for doing around 100mph - very silly, I didn`t get there any quicker

ISOMETRIC

Step by step guide using Isometric technique

Once again there is no obvious choice so we have elected to use the Isometric technique.

This is the actual house. Semi detached with an integral garage and a handy little porch. Very nice house and exceptional value for money.

AS ALWAYS START WITH BASIC OUTLINE

- get the outline first

This is an isometric study - just using your drawing board and set square to draw exact lines in scale.

As before, if it helps, draw the box first to the correct size and then shape the building within the box or probably better to add the roof later.

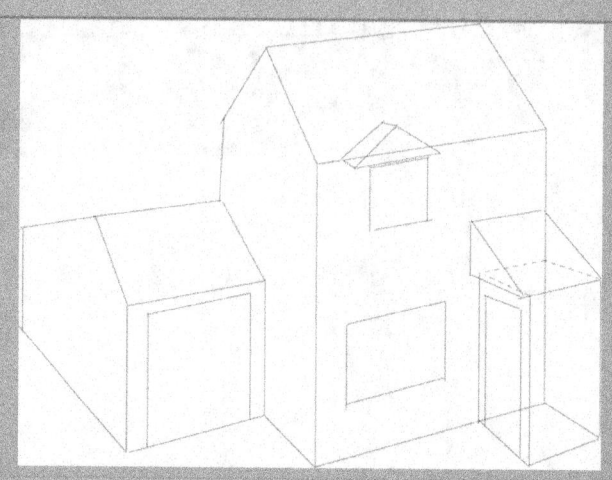

START ADDING FEATURES
KEEP IT LIGHT

REFINE THE DETAIL

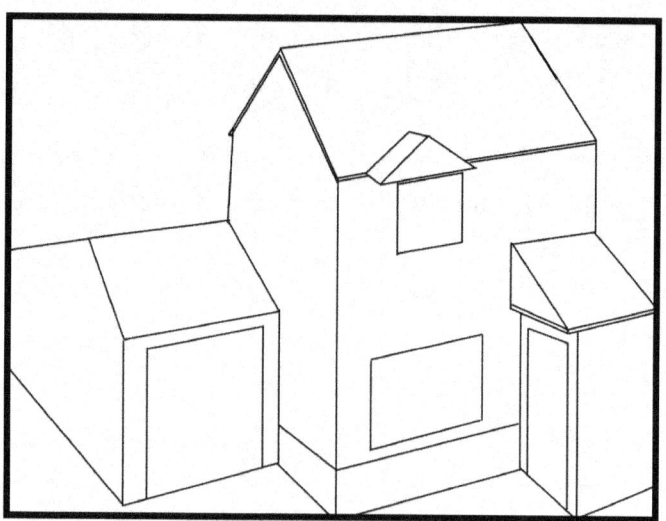

WITH EXTRA FEATURES

PROJECT STUDY C

CHAPTER 4

4 BED DETACHED
Probably the cosiest estate in Stoke
Less than half the price of our similar house in Horley

This is our most recent house which we acquired for my
elderly mother and subsequently inherited.

Nicely designed and well presented house with a lot of potential for
conversion. We also used this house as a study for the Granny Flat.

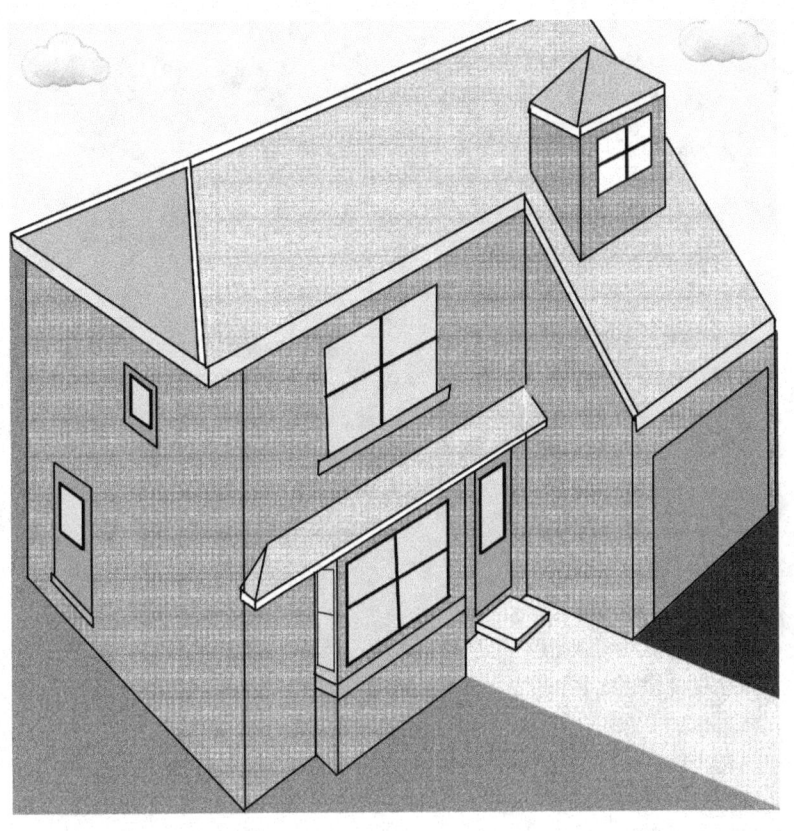

STEP BY STEP GUIDE

OUR HOUSE IN STOKE ON TRENT
AXONOMETRIC
3D STUDY

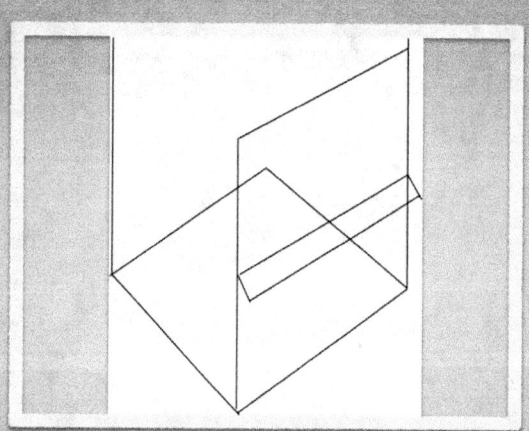

AS USUAL START WITH A BOX
THEN ADD DETAILS TO THE BOX

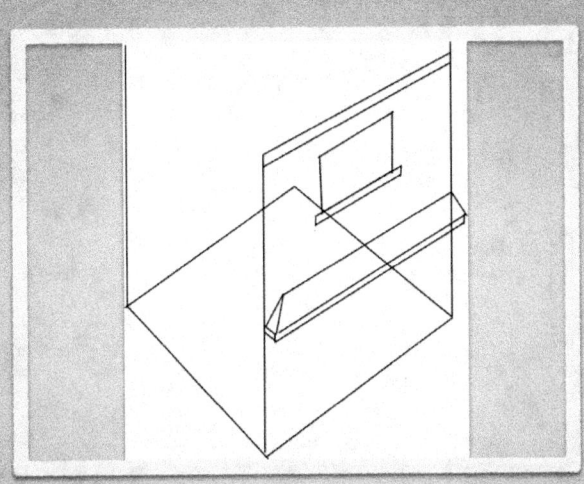

add more detail

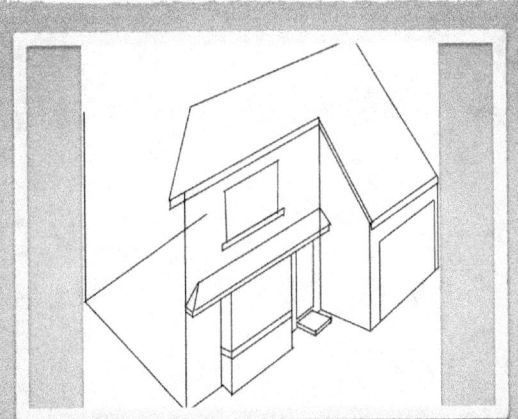

beginning to look like a house

it is a house

getting down to finer detail

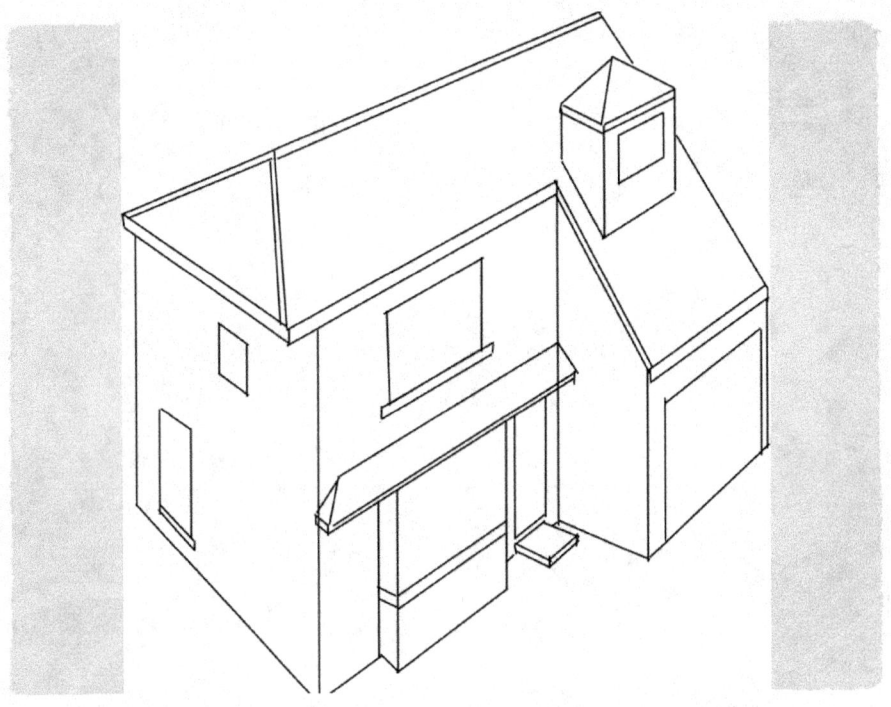

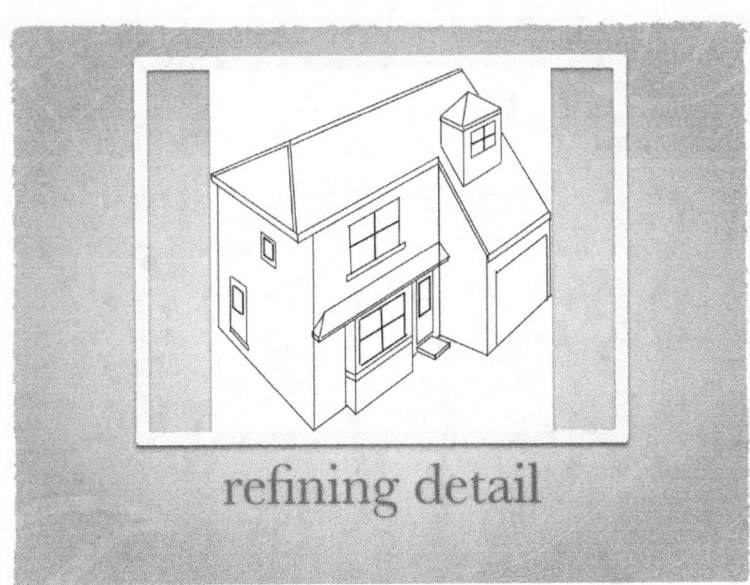

refining detail

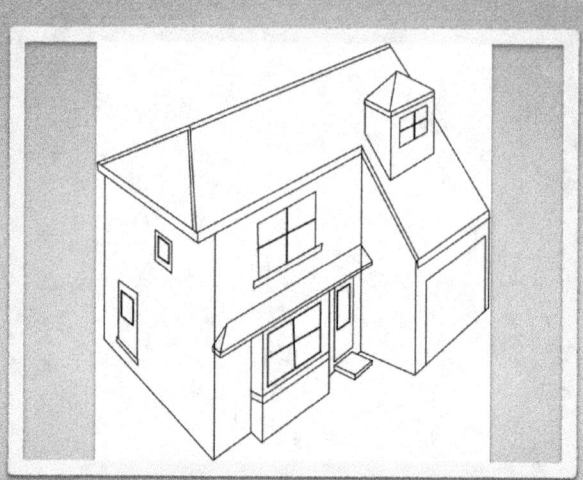

tidying the drawing
ready to render

PROJECT STUDY D

OUR MOTEL NEAR KIRRIEMUIR

* *Part of the RJA Hotel /Motel complex*
* *14-16 rooms all en suite*
* *now demolished to make way for new housing*

We purchased the Hotel with Motel around 1980. The motel had only been built about 5 years before but was not of a good standard and used to freeze solid during the winter months. We rebranded the Motel as a stand alone business and marketed it separately from the Hotel.

These drawings represent some of the ideas to enhance the look and facilities of the unit and especially clean up the exterior so that it could be redecorated easily.

THE MAIN BUILDING

THE HOTEL IS IN THE BACKGROUND

THIS IS THE BUILDING AS WAS

THE NEW DESIGN WILL BE A FACE LIFT

START WITH A BOX

FIX THE VANISHING POINTS AND HORIZON LINE

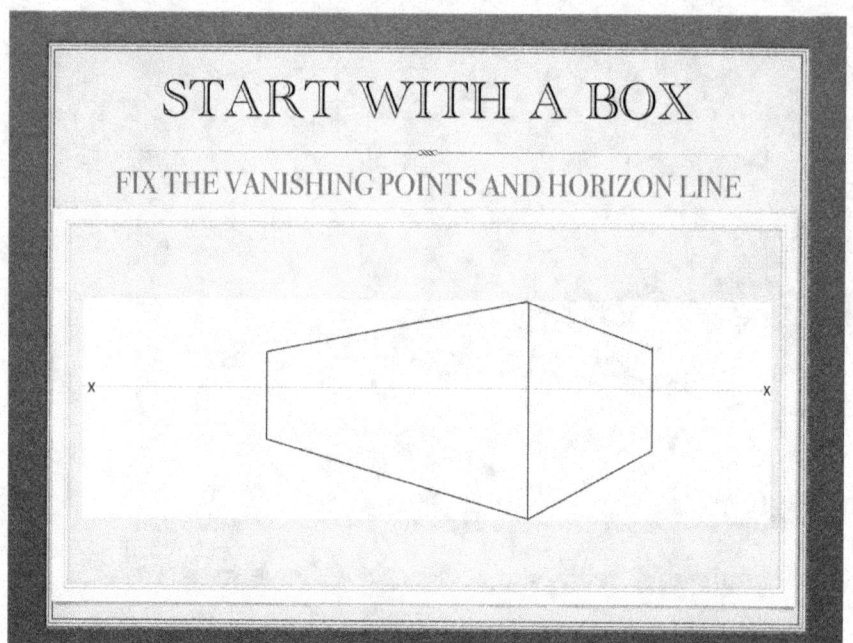

ADD DETAIL

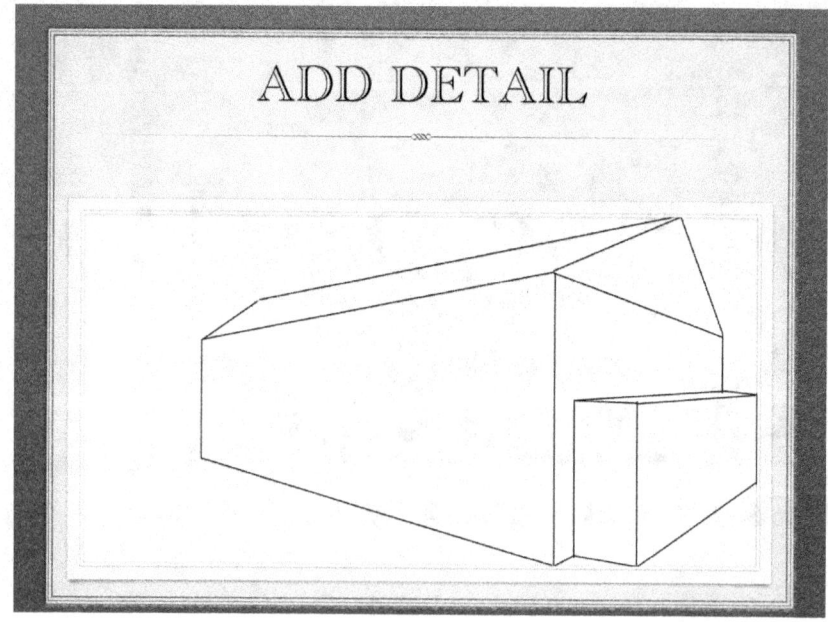

ADD ROOF TO PORCH

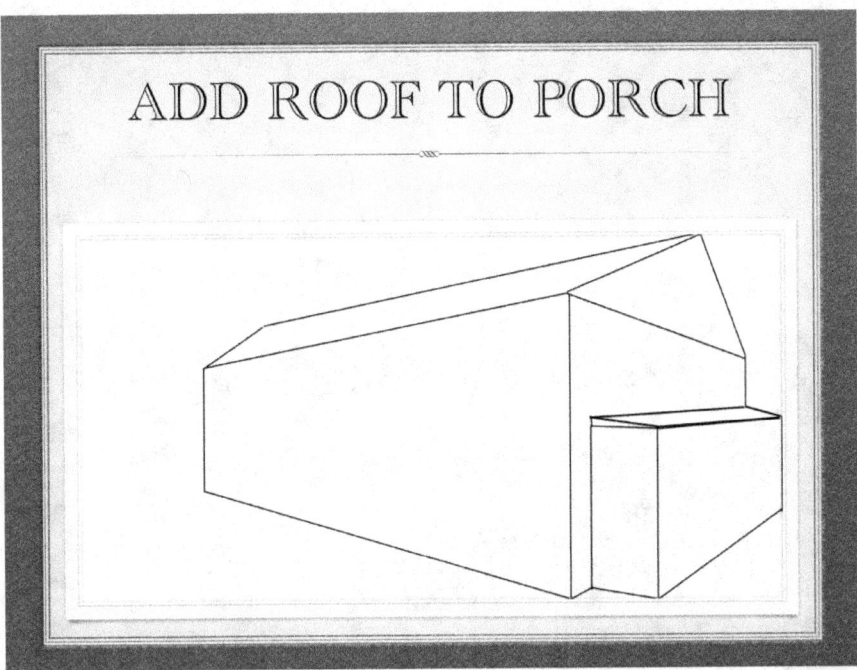

MORE DETAILS

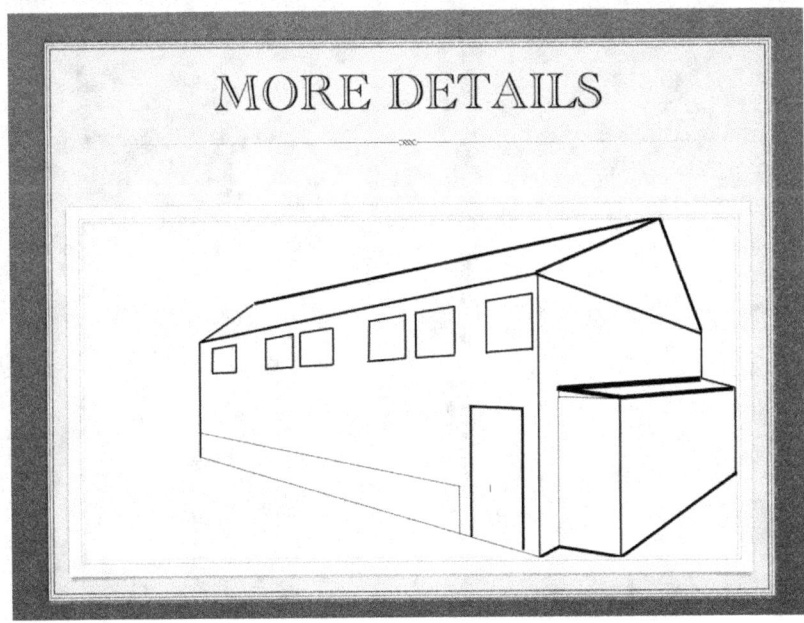

PLAN A PROPOSAL

NEW SIGN

TAKING SHAPE

CHAPTER 6

PROJECT STUDY E

BOUGHTON MONCHELSEA

❖ *This lovely old stately home was in the Rider family for around 200 years before it was squandered away by one of my forebears*

The building has a long history and as far as we know, has not had any extensions or major alterations over the last years. It used to be open to the public and on our first visit my mother spied a painting on the stairs which was virtually my identical twin.

Further investigation showed that it was once owned by a branch of the Rider family. We asked if they would give it back but they weren`t interested.

STEP BY STEP

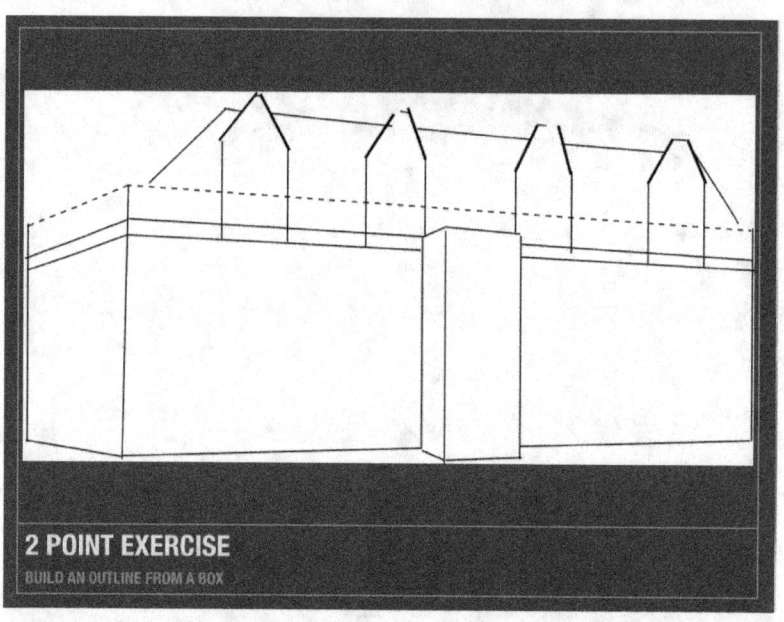

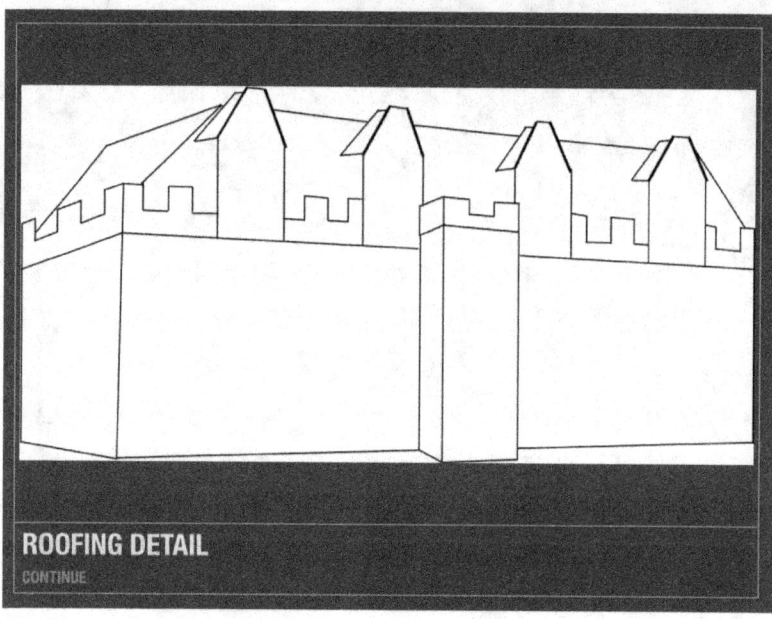

ADD WINDOWS
FRONT OF BUILDING

OPEN THE PLAN
TO ADD SURROUNDING DETAIL

PRESENTATION A

2 point perspective is eminently suitable for this study as it would be for any large project.

The extra detail also enhances the presentation and consequent appeal to the client.

CENTRE ST.
A CANADIAN STUDY

We acquired the house in 1953 and these images show some of the developments up until 1956 when we left Canada to return to England for the first time.

When we moved in the house was a bit of a wreck. It had been llived in by the mother of a friend of my parents and had been left to decay. to be fair we got the property at a bargain price and with a built in mortgage but it needed renovating from top to basement.

Luckily Dad was more than a handyman he was a handy craftsman and could turn his hand to virtually anything and everything with equally professional results.

The works involved installing a new boiler with hot air distribution and copious high pressure water.

STARTING BUILDING

- *we started at the front and this is me and my sister getting stuck in with building the new porch and tidying up the front garden.*
- *next came the kitchen*
- *then the roof*
- *then the living and dining rooms*
- *then the bedroom*
- *then the bathroom*
- *then we gave up*

Dad renewed all the electrics which were also centred in the cellar. I hate cellars but they held a lot o junk. We never got around to making it a dream cellar with games room et al.

We also had an old original scullery to the rear of the house which had the original hand pump for the water. We tended to use this for junk and never took it any further.

Dad also installed one of the first directionable antennae in the town and we had one of the first large screen TV's in the town. Well before many of the more affluent people in the area. One flaw however, during the very cold mid Ontario winters the aerial froze for many days at a time and we burnt the motor out trying to thaw it out. When it froze it often got stuck in the wrong place so we couldn't really receive much of a signal from aywhere. The best signal we got was from Buffalo New York which was about 400 miles away.

We used to revel in Batman. Dagwood and Blondie and the Ozzie and Harriet Nelson show with the, then very young Ricky Nelson. Before that I listened to 'The Shadow' on our phonograph. Great days.

For this exercise I have managed to acquire some images of the house as it has been developed and we are going to study the layout and improvements we made plus a few improvements that never quite got off the ground. Still for a North American house it has had quite a good innings.

Apart from the obvious plan views which are fairly traditional I have decided to do the ground floor study in a Bird's Eye technique.

As before and with the other techniques we have used throughout this guide you will need to be familiar with all the 3d techniques if you are to produce the exercises. You can find all of the 3d drawing techniques in our Mini Guide series 2016. Just search for the guide you want.

You can also contact us via our website if you need any assistance and with all the guides we produce we offer unlimited on line support for anyone purchasing our guides.

As the final exercise which is not shown as an example we would ask you to draw the first floor using the bird's eye technique plus the whole house exterior using any technique you feel is suitable. If you wish we can provide individual critique on any of your presentations. Contact us via our website to receive uploading details.

The house-1953 with completed porch

Outline plan

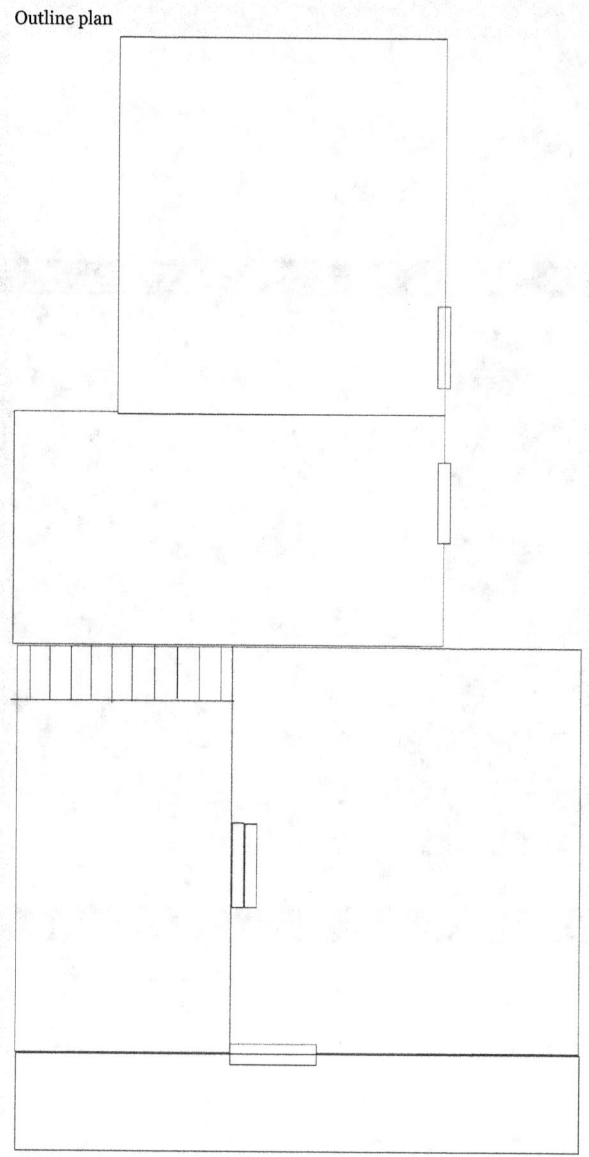

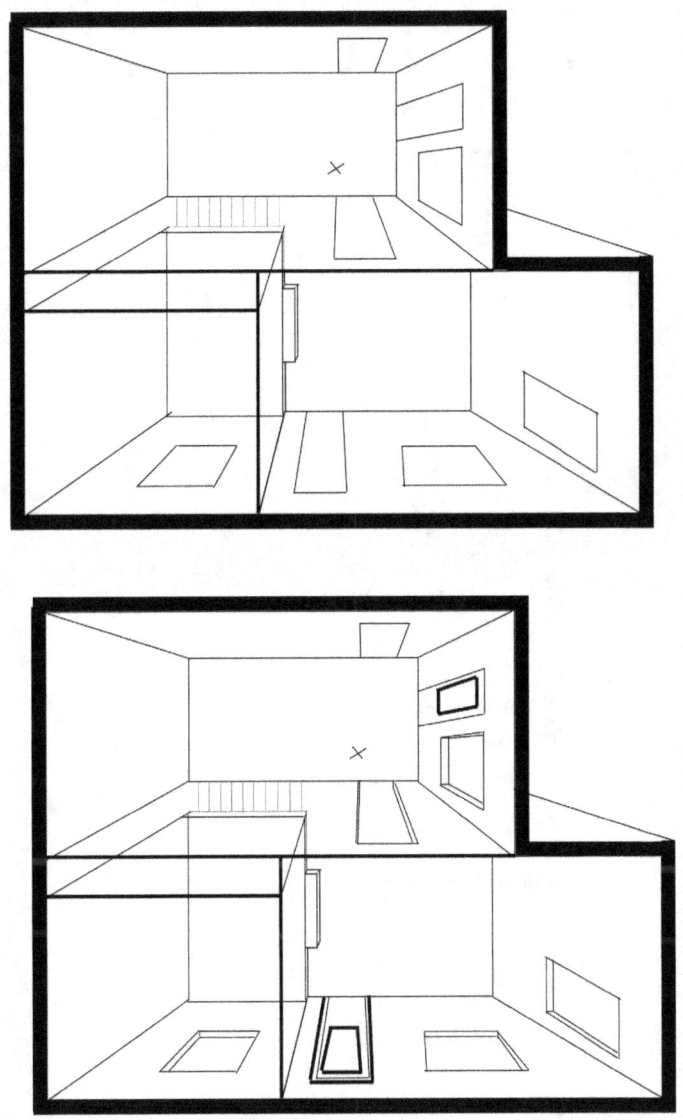

New Plan

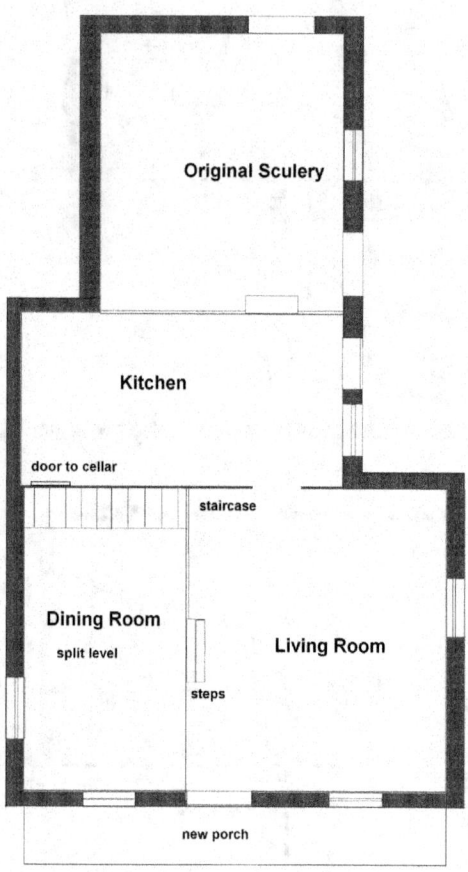

Original Sculery

Kitchen

door to cellar

staircase

Dining Room

split level

steps

Living Room

new porch

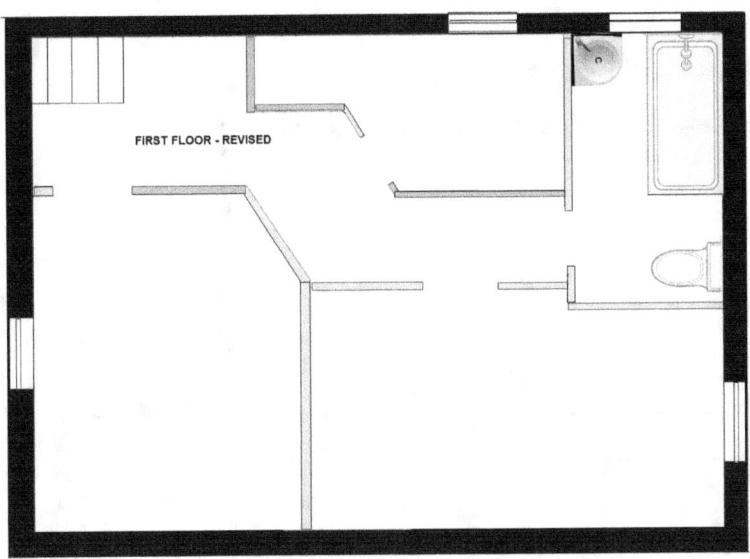

FIRST FLOOR - REVISED

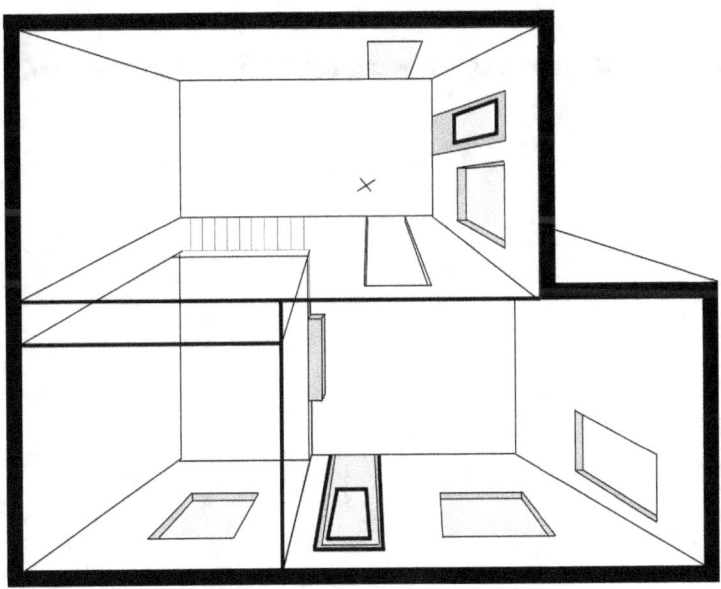

Bird's Eye Study of Centre St.

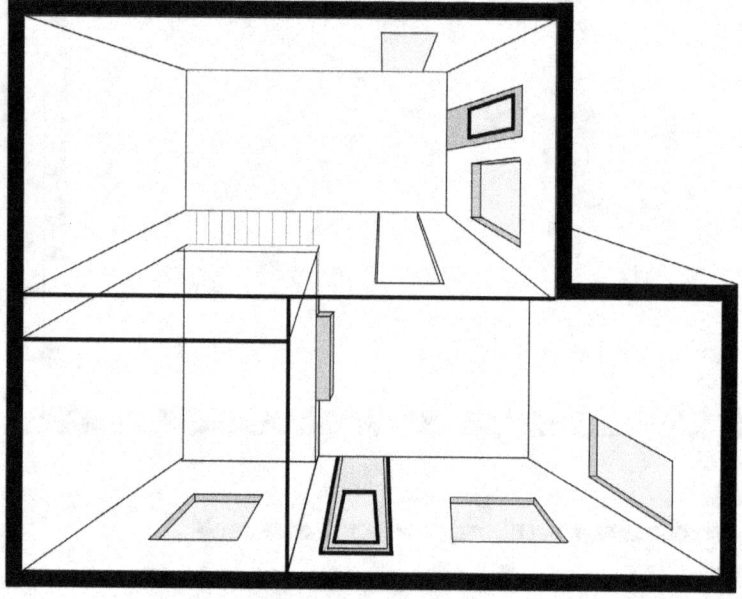

House in 2015

House in 1956

New bathroom

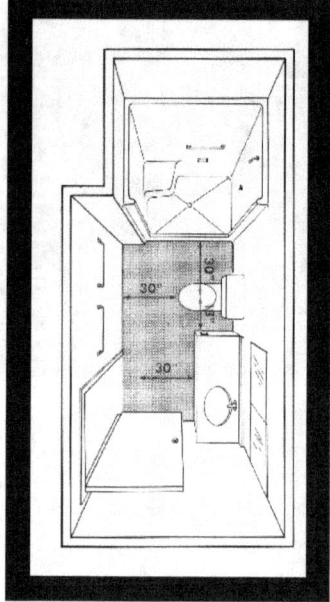

WPS

CHAPTER 8

*TO CLOSE OUR STUDIES WHAT BEST THAN TO
LOOK AT MY OLD ALMA MATER IN CANADA.*

A lovely old Victorian building which had a lot of life left in her
but is now no more. We can celebrate in pictures.

Public School — Wingham, Ont.